Quick Start Guides

I0177391

The Essential
MEDITERRANEAN
DIET
Recipe Book

Easy Cooking for
Weight Loss, Good
Health & Longevity

Delicious Calorie-Counted Recipes For Healthy Eating.

First published in 2020 by Erin Rose Publishing

Text and illustration copyright © 2020 Erin Rose Publishing

Design: Julie Anson

ISBN: 978-1-9161523-8-0

A CIP record for this book is available from the British Library.

DISCLAIMER: This book is for informational purposes only and not intended as a substitute for the medical advice, diagnosis or treatment of a physician or qualified healthcare provider. The reader should consult a physician before undertaking a new health care regime and in all matters relating to his/her health, and particularly with respect to any symptoms that may require diagnosis or medical attention.

While every care has been taken in compiling the recipes for this book we cannot accept responsibility for any problems which arise as a result of preparing one of the recipes. The author and publisher disclaim responsibility for any adverse effects that may arise from the use or application of the recipes in this book. Some of the recipes in this book include nuts. If you have a nut allergy it's important to avoid these.

CONTENTS

Introduction..1

The Benefits Of The Mediterranean Diet 2

Getting Started 3

Recipes

BREAKFASTS 5

Creamy Orange Smoothie 6

Cherry & Raspberry Smoothie......................................7

Berry Smoothie 8

Chocolatey Smoothie 9

Pink Grapefruit Smoothie 10

Creamy Nut Butter Smoothie.....................................11

Pear & Avocado Smoothie 12

Parmesan & Herb Scramble 13

Chicken, Avocado & Basil Omelette 14

Feta & Courgette Omelette 15

Cheese, Herb & Olive Frittata....................................16

Cheese & Tomato Mug Omelette................................17

LIGHT BITES 19

Chicken & Avocado Wraps..20

Chorizo Scramble 21

Cheese & Spinach Slice 22

Courgette (Zucchini) Fritters 23

Goats' Cheese Stuffed Cherry Tomatoes 24

Asparagus & Red Pepper Sauce 25

Smoked Paprika Chicken & Green Peppers...................26

Prawn, Crab & Avocado Wraps 27

Halloumi Salad 28

Serrano & Rocket Salad...29

Prawn, Avocado & Cannellini Salad 30

Spiced Chicken & Courgette..31

Tuna & Bean Salad..32

Greek Chicken Salad 33

Feta Cheese & Butterbean Salad 34

Chicken & Chorizo Kebabs 35

Asparagus & Poached Egg 36

Paprika Prawn Tapas 37

Mozzarella & Cauliflower Bake..38

Pesto & Bacon Stuffed Mushrooms 39

Parmesan Asparagus...40

Basil & Lemon Hummus With Celery...41

Oven Roasted Tomatoes & Feta Cheese 42

Basil & Tomato Olives 43

Carrot & Basil Soup...44

Quick Chicken & Red Pepper Soup...45

Tomato & Pesto Soup...46

Quick Chicken & Asparagus Soup 47

Fennel & Broccoli Soup 48

Quick Bean & Parmesan Soup 49

Beef & Mushroom Soup 50

Creamy Red Pepper Soup 51

Vegetable & Chorizo Soup 52

Asparagus Soup..53

Broccoli & Cheese Soup 54

MAIN MEALS 55

Salmon & Pomegranate Salsa.................................56

Tomato & Herb Stuffed Chicken..............................57

Spicy Meatballs & Yogurt Dip 58

Mustard Turkey & Mashed Butter Beans 59

Slow Cooked Chicken Cacciatore............................60

Roast Lemon & Herb Chicken 61

Tomato & Courgette (Zucchini) Bake 62

Lemon & Almond Crumbed Prawns 63

Paprika Pork Skewers..64

Turkey & Chickpea Balls 65

Chorizo Stir-Fry 66

Slow-Cooked Ratatouille......................................67

Spiced Citrus & Olive Pork 68

Smoked Salmon & Pesto 'Spaghetti' 69

Tuna Casserole 70

Halloumi Skewers 71

Fried Avocados 72

Slow Cooked Beans & Pancetta 73

Chicken, Chorizo & Vegetable Casserole 74

Roasted Sardines With Herb Crust 75

Pulled Chicken Wraps...76

Sundried Tomato Stuffed Chicken 77

Balsamic Roast Vegetables...................................78

Cod With Tomato & Olives 79

Rosemary Chicken & Roast Vegetables 80

Tomato & Pesto Chicken 81

Spiced Quinoa & Chickpea Falafels........................82

Broccoli & Bean Bites..83

Sirloin Steak & Garlic Prawns 84

Halloumi, Pine Nut & Vegetable Bake 85

Lemon Salmon & Spinach...86

Mushroom Stuffed Peppers 87

Mozzarella & Aubergine Bake..88

SWEET TREATS...89

Macadamia & Chocolate Yogurt 90

Chocolate Cashew Truffles 91

Vanilla Mug Cake..92

Banana Frappuccino 93

Pistachio & Raspberry Fool 94

Whipped Yogurt, Apples & Walnuts...95

INTRODUCTION

Are you ready to lose weight and boost your vitality on the Mediterranean Diet, then look no further! This easy-to-use cookbook is filled with delicious, tantalising Mediterranean-style recipes for weight loss.

You can get started straight away with tasty recipes to trim your waistline, help you shed unwanted pounds and boost your health and longevity.

The simple, calorie-counted, recipes in this **Quick Start Guide** are also low in carbohydrates and they're packed with health-boosting nutrients so you can reap all the benefits of one of the world's best all-round diets.

You can enjoy delicious fresh ingredients on a diet which is rich in fruits, vegetables, beans, nuts, fish, olive oil, herbs and spices. Even though the diet differs slightly in the various Mediterranean countries, studies have shown these countries have lower rates of chronic diseases and longer life expectancy.

The Mediterranean diet is recognised by the medical profession as having major benefits and it's advised to be followed for protection against heart disease, diabetes and inflammatory conditions, depression and dementia.

So, whether you wish to lose weight, prevent ill health or simply enjoy eating healthily, you can get started with lots of simple, easy, recipes which are also calorie-counted, so if you also wish to restrict calories, you can!

the Benefits Of the Mediterranean Diet

Probably the most well-known aspect of the Mediterranean diet is the emphasis on eating healthy fats. Olive oil contains antioxidants and it's also anti-inflammatory, offering protection against diabetes and cardiovascular disease. Healthy fats, such as those from fatty fish like salmon or olive oil and nuts, reduce the risk of type 2 diabetes.

Healthy, whole foods, such as fruit, vegetables contain antioxidants which are can slow down ageing, improve cognitive function, chronic illnesses, reduce stress and inflammation and improve life expectancy. The whole foods in the Mediterranean diet make it a sensible way of eating for most people who wish to enjoy good health as long as possible.

Healthy fats are not only great for you, they are essential. Research has shown the Mediterranean diet is effective in reducing cardiovascular disease, improving blood sugar and reducing the Body Mass Index (BMI) which is great news when you can enjoy nutritious avocados, nuts and fish.

The benefits of the Mediterranean diet are widely accepted, however it doesn't extend to eating heaps of pasta and starchy carbohydrates like bread. These are best avoided as this will help you kick any food cravings and overcome difficulty losing weight due to metabolic syndrome and blood sugar imbalance. Avoiding starchy and sugary foods will help prevent blood sugar fluctuations, reduce cravings and help with weight loss. The recipes in the book will help you get the most out of the Mediterranean diet, avoid the pitfalls and fuel your body with lots of delicious foods which will help you feel satisfied and prevent hunger pangs, whilst you lose weight.

Getting Started

You can begin by deciding what you wish to achieve on the Mediterranean diet. Do you wish to improve your health or do you wish to lose more weight and restrict calories? Check out some recipes before stocking up on your store cupboard essentials.

Try to avoid processed food and starchy or refined carbohydrates and sugars. Cooking your meals yourself will help you to avoid hidden sugars, balance blood sugar and will prevent hunger.

Eat plenty of vegetables and fruit 7-10 portions a day is ideal. Use olive oil as a replacement for unhealthy fats and margarine.

This cookbook also contains recipes for healthier, low-carb, low-calorie desserts, however only eat these in moderation and avoid them completely if you have sugar cravings. These can be reduced or eliminated completely by avoiding sugar and starchy carbohydrates.

You can substitute pasta, spaghetti, rice, bread or potatoes for lower carbohydrate alternatives instead, such as; vegetables, heaps of salad, beans or pulses. Substitute rice for cauliflower 'rice' which can be adapted to suit your main course by adding herbs, spices or vegetables.

Chocolate bars, sweets and candies can be swapped for good quality 100% cocoa powder or cacao nibs can be added to recipes

If you check out the ingredients list on processed soups you may realise they should be excluded from your diet due to excess carb/sugar content. Don't let preparation time put you off making your own soups. You can make a large batch and refrigerate or freeze them which will save you time in the long run.

Be careful of flavoured yogurts – they can have large amounts of sugar added. However plain or Greek yogurt is a great addition to your diet and you can get creative by adding, ground nuts, seeds, cocoa powder or a small amount of chopped fruit.

Avoid or reduce your intake of starchy carbohydrates, such as:

- Pasta
- Bread
- Pizza
- Biscuits
- Pastries

- Cakes
- Muesli
- Cookies
- Crackers
- Rice cakes

- Oat cakes
- Noodles
- Rice
- Potatoes
- Sugary foods and drinks.

Foods You Can Enjoy

- Fish, shellfish, chicken, lamb, turkey, beef, pork.

- Eggs

- Beans and pulses

- Dairy produce

- Fresh fruit and vegetables

- Fresh herbs and spices

- Olive oil, avocado oil and nut oils

Always seek your doctor's advice before making any radical dietary changes, especially if have a medical condition, underlying health issues, are convalescing or are pregnant.

BREAKFASTS

Creamy Orange Smoothie

SERVES 1

144 calories per serving

Ingredients

50g (2oz) plain Greek yogurt

1 medium orange, peeled

1 pear, cored

½ honeydew melon, flesh only

Method

Place all of the ingredients into a blender and add just enough water to cover them. Blitz until smooth. Pour and enjoy!

Cherry & Raspberry Smoothie

Ingredients

25g (1oz) frozen raspberries

6 cherries, de-stoned

1 apple, cored

1/2 cantaloupe melon, flesh only

SERVES 1

147 calories per serving

Method

Place all the ingredients into a blender and add just enough water to cover the ingredients. Blitz until smooth. Serve and drink straight away.

Berry Smoothie

Ingredients

50g (2oz) frozen blueberries

50g (2oz) frozen strawberries

125g (4oz) plain unflavoured yogurt

100mls (3½ oz) unsweetened soya milk

SERVES 1

162 calories per serving

Method

Whizz the berries, yogurt and soya milk together in a blender and process until smooth.

Chocolatey Smoothie

Ingredients

100g (3½ oz) frozen cherries

1 medjool date

1 tablespoon cocoa powder

2 teaspoons chia seeds

200mls (7fl oz) almond milk (or other milk alternative)

A small handful of fresh spinach (optional)

SERVES 1

239 calories per serving

Method

Place all the ingredients into a blender and process until smooth and creamy.

Pink Grapefruit Smoothie

Ingredients

1 carrot, peeled

2.5cm (1 inch) chunk of root ginger, peeled

1 pink grapefruit, peeled

SERVES 1

159 calories per serving

Method

Place all of the ingredients into a blender with sufficient water to just cover the ingredients. Blitz until smooth. Serve with a few ice cubes and enjoy.

Creamy Nut Butter Smoothie

Ingredients

1 medium banana, peeled

1 teaspoon almond butter

1 tablespoon natural Greek yogurt

200mls (7fl oz) almond milk

SERVES 1

284 calories per serving

Method

Place all the ingredients into a blender and process until smooth and creamy. Serve with a few ice cubes and drink straight away.

Pear & Avocado Smoothie

Ingredients

1 small handful of fresh spinach

1 pear, core removed

1/2 teaspoon of spirulina powder (optional)

Flesh of 1/2 avocado

**SERVES
1**

192
calories
per serving

Method

Place the ingredients into a blender and pour in just enough cold water to cover them. Blitz until smooth and creamy. Serve and drink.

Parmesan & Herb Scramble

Ingredients

2 eggs

1 tablespoon crème fraîche

1 tablespoon grated Parmesan cheese

1 teaspoon fresh oregano, chopped

1 teaspoon fresh basil leaves, chopped

1 teaspoon butter

1/2 teaspoon mixed herbs (optional)

SERVES 1

204 calories per serving

Method

Crack the eggs into a bowl, whisk them up. Add in the Parmesan cheese, crème fraîche, basil, oregano and mixed herbs (if using). Heat the butter in a frying pan. Pour in the egg mixture and stir constantly until the eggs are scrambled and set. Serve and enjoy.

Chicken, Avocado & Basil Omelette

Ingredients

25g (1oz) Cheddar cheese, grated (shredded)

50g (2oz) chicken leftovers, chopped

2 eggs, beaten

Flesh of ½ avocado, chopped

1 teaspoon fresh basil

1 teaspoon olive oil

Freshly ground black pepper

SERVES 1

491 calories per serving

Method

Heat the olive oil in a frying pan then pour in the beaten egg mixture. While it begins to set sprinkle on the grated cheese, basil, chicken and chopped avocado. Cook until the eggs are completely set and the cheese has melted. Season with black pepper.

Feta & Courgette Omelette

Ingredients

25g (1oz) feta cheese, crumbled

2 eggs

1 small courgette (zucchini), grated (shredded)

1 teaspoon fresh parsley, chopped

1 tablespoon olive oil

SERVES 1

337 calories per serving

Method

Place the eggs in a bowl and whisk them. Stir in the cheese and courgette (zucchini). Heat the olive oil in a frying pan. Pour in the egg mixture and cook until it is set. Sprinkle with parsley and serve.

Cheese, Herb & Olive Frittata

SERVES 2

229
calories
per serving

Ingredients

25g (1oz) mozzarella cheese, grated (shredded)

25g (1oz) pitted black olives, halved

4 eggs

4 cherry tomatoes, halved

1 tablespoon fresh parsley, chopped

1 tablespoon fresh basil, chopped

2 teaspoons olive oil

Method

Whisk the eggs in a bowl and add in the parsley, basil, olives and tomatoes. Stir in the cheese and stir it. Heat the oil in a small frying pan and pour in the egg mixture. Cook the egg mixture for around 3 minutes or until it completely sets. You can finish it off under a hot grill (broiler) if you wish. Gently remove it from the pan and cut it into two. You can easily double the quantity of ingredients and store the extra portions to be eaten cold.

Cheese & Tomato Mug Omelette

Ingredients

25g (1oz) mozzarella cheese

2 cherry tomatoes, chopped

2 eggs

2 teaspoons chopped red pepper (bell pepper)

1/4 teaspoon dried oregano

1/2 teaspoon softened butter

SERVES 1

221 calories per serving

Method

Crack the eggs into a large mug and beat them. Add in the remaining ingredients. Place the mug in a microwave and cook on full power for 30 seconds. Stir and return it to the microwave for another 30 seconds, stir and cook for another 30-60 seconds or until the egg is set. As a variation try adding cooked sausage, bacon, chicken, chorizo and spring onions (scallions). Or you can simply go for plain eggs as a quick and easy alternative to scrambling.

LIGHT
BITES

Chicken & Avocado Wraps

Ingredients

50g (2oz) cooked kidney beans, rinsed and drained

1 cooked chicken breast, finely chopped

1/4 cucumber, peeled, deseeded and chopped

Flesh of 1/2 avocado

Juice 1/4 lemon

1 teaspoon olive oil

4 little gem lettuce leaves

SERVES 1

444
calories
per serving

Method

Place the avocado, olive oil and lemon juice in a food processor and mix until smooth and creamy. Put the chicken, kidney beans and cucumber in a bowl and add the avocado mixture. Stir it well to combine it. Scoop some of the mixture into each of the lettuce leaves. Eat straight away.

Chorizo Scramble

Ingredients

25g (1oz) chorizo sausage, chopped

25g (1oz) cheese, grated (shredded)

2 eggs, beaten

1 teaspoon butter

**SERVES
1**

375
calories
per serving

Method

Heat the butter in a frying pan and add in the chorizo. Cook for around 2 minutes. Pour in the beaten egg and stir, scrambling the eggs until completely cooked. Serve onto a plate and sprinkle with grated (shredded) cheese.

Cheese & Spinach Slice

Ingredients

225g (8oz) mozzarella cheese, grated (shredded)

120g (4oz) ground almonds

25g (1oz) fresh spinach leaves, chopped

2 eggs

1 onion, finely chopped

1 teaspoon baking powder

200mls (7fl oz) almond milk

SERVES 4

390 calories per serving

Method

Place the spinach into a saucepan, cover it with warm water, bring it to the boil and cook for 3 minutes. Drain it and set aside. Place the ground almonds in a bowl and add in the eggs, milk and baking powder and mix well. Add in the chopped onion, spinach and cheese and combine the mixture. Spoon the mixture into an ovenproof dish and smooth it out. Transfer it to the oven and bake at 190C/375F for 35 minutes. Cut into slices before serving.

Courgette (Zucchini) Fritters

Ingredients

450g (1lb) courgettes (zucchinis), grated (shredded)

100g (3½ oz) Parmesan cheese

3 cloves of garlic

3 spring onions (scallions), chopped

2 eggs, beaten

1 teaspoon dried mixed herbs

1 tablespoon olive oil

Sprinkling of salt

SERVES 4

204 calories per serving

Method

Place the grated (shredded) courgette (zucchini) into a colander and sprinkle with a little salt. Allow it to sit for 30 minutes then squeeze out any excess moisture. Place the eggs, Parmesan, spring onions (scallions), garlic and dried herbs into a bowl and mix well with the courgettes. Scoop out a spoonful of the mixture and shape it into patties. Heat the oil in a frying pan, add the patties and cook for 2 minutes, turn them over and cook for another 2 minutes. Serve warm.

Goats' Cheese Stuffed Cherry Tomatoes

Ingredients

125g (4oz) goats' cheese

24 cherry tomatoes, halved

1/2 teaspoon salt

1/2 teaspoon freshly ground black pepper

Small handful fresh basil, very finely chopped

SERVES 4

120 calories per serving

Method

Place the goats' cheese in a bowl and mix in the chopped basil. Season with salt and black pepper. Gently scoop the tomato seeds and pulp out from inside the tomatoes and pour out any juice. Using a teaspoon scoop some of the cheese mixture into each tomato. Place them on a decorative plate and serve.

Asparagus & Red Pepper Sauce

Ingredients

25g (1oz) ground almonds (almond meal/almond flour)

14 stalks of asparagus, tough part of stalk removed

6 spring onions (scallions)

1 red pepper (bell pepper), halved and deseeded

1/4 teaspoon chilli powder

2 tablespoons water

1 tablespoon olive oil

Juice of 1/2 lemon

Sea salt

SERVES 2

177 calories per serving

Method

Heat the oil in a griddle pan or frying pan. Add the asparagus and spring onions (scallions). Cook until they have softened, turning occasionally. In the meantime, place the red pepper (bell pepper), chilli powder, almonds, water and lemon juice into a blender and blitz until smooth. Serve the asparagus and spring onions onto plates and serve the sauce on the side.

Smoked Paprika Chicken & Green Peppers

Ingredients

2 chicken breasts, chopped

2 cloves of garlic, chopped

2 handfuls of rocket (arugula) leaves

1 green peppers (bell peppers)

1 onion, peeled and chopped

1 teaspoon smoked paprika

2 teaspoons olive oil

Sea salt

Freshly ground black

SERVES 2

241 calories per serving

Method

Place the chicken in a bowl and sprinkle on the smoked paprika. Heat the oil in a large frying pan. Add the chicken and cook for around 3 minutes. Add in the onion, garlic and peppers and cook until the vegetables have softened. Scatter the rocket (arugula) on a plate and serve the chicken and vegetables on top. Season with salt and pepper. Eat straight away.

Prawn, Crab & Avocado Wraps

Ingredients

75g (3oz) peeled cooked prawns (shrimps)
75g (3oz) cooked crabmeat
2 spring onions (scallions) chopped
1 tomato, chopped
1 little gem lettuce
1/2 avocado, de-stoned, peeled and diced
2 teaspoons mayonnaise
Squeeze of lemon juice
Small handful of chives, chopped
Wedge of lemon
Sea salt
Freshly ground black pepper

SERVES 1

391
calories
per serving

Method

Place the mayonnaise and lemon juice in a bowl and mix well. Season with salt and pepper. Add the prawns, crabmeat, spring onions (scallions) and tomato into the mixture and stir. Separate the lettuce leaves and lay them onto a plate. Scatter some of the diced avocado into each lettuce leaf. Spoon some of the prawn mixture into each lettuce leaf. Sprinkle some chopped chives into each lettuce leaf. Chill before serving.

Halloumi Salad

Ingredients

450g (1lb) asparagus, tough end removed

250g (9 oz) halloumi cheese, cut into slices

2 large handfuls of spinach leaves

1 tablespoon olive oil

Sea salt

Freshly ground black pepper

SERVES 4

257 calories per serving

Method

Heat the olive oil in a frying pan and cook the asparagus for 4 minutes or until tender. Remove, set aside and keep warm. Place the halloumi in the frying pan and cook for 2 minutes on each side until golden. Serve the spinach leaves onto plates and add the asparagus and halloumi slices. Season with salt and pepper.

Serrano & Rocket Salad

Ingredients

150g (5oz) Serrano ham

1 large handful of spinach leaves

1 large handful of rocket (arugula leaves)

1 tablespoons olive oil

1 tablespoon apple cider vinegar

1 tablespoon fresh orange juice

SERVES 2

224
calories
per serving

Method

Pour the oil, vinegar and juice into a bowl and toss the spinach and rocket (arugula) leaves in the mixture. Serve the leaves onto plates and place the ham on top.

Prawn, Avocado & Cannellini Salad

Ingredients

200g (7oz) cooked king prawns (shrimps)
150g (5oz) tinned cannellini beans
2 large handfuls of spinach leaves
1 avocado, peeled, de-stoned and chopped
1 teaspoon fresh coriander (cilantro) leaves, chopped
1/2 cucumber, chopped
1/2 teaspoon chilli powder
1/2 teaspoon paprika
Zest and juice of 1 lime
1 tablespoon olive oil

SERVES 2

373 calories per serving

Method

Place the prawns into a bowl and sprinkle on the paprika and mix well. Place the chilli, lime juice and zest and oil in a bowl and stir well. Add in the cannellini beans, avocado, cucumber and coriander (cilantro) and toss them in the dressing. Serve the spinach onto plates and add the tossed salad with the prawns on top.

Spiced Chicken & Courgette Salad

Ingredients

50g (2oz) chagrilled artichokes in oil, drained and chopped

2 chicken breasts, cut into strips

2 medium courgettes (zucchini), sliced lengthways

2 large handfuls of rocket (arugula) leaves

2 teaspoons olive oil

2 teaspoons balsamic vinegar

1 teaspoon harissa paste

SERVES 1

314 calories per serving

Method

Place the harissa paste and olive oil in a bowl and coat the chicken breasts in the mixture. Heat a griddle pan on a high heat. Place the courgette (zucchini) slices on the pan and cook until they have softened. Set them aside and keep warm. Add the chicken to the pan and cook it for around 6 minutes or until it's completely cooked, turning it over halfway through. Scatter the rocket (arugula) leaves onto a plate together with the artichoke pieces. Add the courgette and chicken to the salad. Drizzle the balsamic vinegar and serve.

Tuna & Bean Salad

Ingredients

3 tablespoons lemon juice

1 tablespoon olive oil

1 clove garlic, chopped

250g (9oz) cannellini beans, drained and rinsed

250g (9oz) tinned tuna

1 onion, finely chopped

1 tablespoon fresh parsley, chopped

SERVES 2

352 calories per serving

Method

Place the lemon juice, olive oil, garlic and garlic into a bowl and stir well. Add the cannellini beans, tuna, onion and parsley to the bowl and coat them in the oil mixture. Serve and eat straight away.

Greek Chicken Salad

Ingredients

75g (3oz) feta cheese, crumbled
50g (2oz) olives
2 tomatoes, chopped
2 cooked chicken breasts, chopped
1 small onion, chopped
1 romaine lettuce, chopped
1/2 cucumber, peeled and chopped
2 tablespoons apple cider vinegar
2 tablespoons extra-virgin olive oil
1 tablespoon fresh oregano, chopped
1 clove of garlic, chopped
Sea salt
Freshly ground black pepper

**SERVES
2**

482
calories
per serving

Method

Place the oil, vinegar, oregano, garlic, salt and pepper into a bowl and mix well. Add the chicken, lettuce, cucumber, tomatoes, olives, onions and feta cheese and coat the ingredients in the oil mixture.

Feta Cheese & Butterbean Salad

Ingredients

400g (14oz) tin of butter beans
250g (9 oz) cherry tomatoes, halved
125g (4oz) feta cheese, crumbled
75g (3oz) black olives, halved
2 tablespoons fresh basil, chopped
2 tablespoons fresh parsley, chopped
1 cucumber, diced
1 red onion, finely sliced
1 yellow pepper (bell pepper), diced
1 tablespoon olive oil
Juice of ½ lemon

SERVES 4

279 calories per serving

Method

Place the olive oil and lemon juice in a bowl and set aside. Place all of the salad ingredients into a large bowl and mix them together. Pour on the dressing and toss the salad ingredients in the mixture.

Chicken & Chorizo Kebabs

Ingredients

250g (10oz) chicken breast, cut into chunks

50g (2oz) chorizo sausage, sliced

8 cherry tomatoes, halved

1 red pepper (bell pepper), cut into chunks

2 teaspoons paprika

Sea salt

Freshly ground black pepper

SERVES 1

325 calories per serving

Method

Sprinkle the chicken with the paprika and season with salt and pepper. Thread the chicken, tomato, pepper and chorizo alternately onto skewers. Place them under a hot grill (broiler) for around 10 minutes or until the chicken is cooked, turning during cooking ensure even cooking.

Asparagus & Poached Egg

Ingredients

150g (5oz) asparagus, tough end removed

50g (2oz) green salad leaves

1 large egg

1 tablespoon olive oil

1 tablespoon lemon juice

Sea salt

Freshly ground black pepper

1 teaspoon parmesan cheese, grated (shredded)

Dash of vinegar

SERVES 1

245 calories per serving

Method

Lay the asparagus under a pre-heated grill and cook for 5 minutes on each side. Half fill a large saucepan with water and bring it to a simmer. Add in the vinegar and stir. Crack the egg into a small side plate and slide it into the water. Cook for around 3 minutes until it firms up but remains soft in the middle. Combine the olive oil and lemon juice in a bowl and season it with salt and pepper. Coat the salad leaves with the dressing. Scatter the salad leaves on a plate, serve the asparagus on top and add the egg. Sprinkle with Parmesan cheese and eat straight away.

Paprika Prawn Tapas

Ingredients

300g (11oz) cooked peeled prawns

150g (5oz) chorizo sausage, chopped

3 garlic cloves, chopped

2 red chillies, deseeded, chopped

1 tablespoon smoked paprika

1 onion, finely chopped

2 tablespoons olive oil

SERVES 1

225 calories per serving

Method

Heat the oil in a frying pan and add in the onion, garlic, chillies and paprika. Cook for 5 minutes until the onions have softened. Add in chorizo and the prawns and cook for 5 minutes. If you are using frozen prawns make sure they are hot right through. Serve by itself or with a leafy green salad.

Mozzarella & Cauliflower Bake

Ingredients

300g (11oz) mozzarella cheese, grated (shredded)

4 eggs

3 cloves of garlic, crushed

2 teaspoons dried oregano

1 cauliflower (approx.700g), grated (shredded)

Sea salt

Freshly ground black pepper

SERVES 8

157 calories per serving

Method

Steam the cauliflower for 5 minutes or until tender and allow it to cool. Place the cauliflower in a bowl and combine it with the eggs, oregano, garlic and two thirds of the cheese. Season with salt and pepper. Grease 2 baking sheets. Divide the mixture in half and place it on the baking sheet and press it into a flat rectangular shape. Transfer the baking sheets to the oven and bake at 220C/440F for 20-25 minutes or until slightly golden. Remove them from the oven and sprinkle them with the remaining mozzarella cheese. Return them to the oven for 4-5 minutes or until the cheese has melted. Enjoy straight away.

Pesto & Bacon Stuffed Mushrooms

Ingredients

125g (4oz) mozzarella, grated (shredded)

125g (4oz) bacon, chopped

8 large mushrooms, cleaned

2 tablespoons basil pesto

2 tablespoons olive oil

SERVES 4

267 calories per serving

Method

Place the mushrooms on a baking tray and pour a little olive oil onto each one. Scatter some of the bacon onto each mushroom and drizzle some pesto sauce onto each one. Top it off with a sprinkling of mozzarella. Place them in the oven at 200C/400F and cook for 8-10 minutes until the cheese is bubbling and hot. Serve with handfuls of leafy greens.

Parmesan Asparagus

Ingredients

200g (7oz) asparagus spears, trimmed

50g (2oz) Parmesan cheese, grated

1 tablespoon olive oil

Freshly ground black pepper

SERVES 2

191 calories per serving

Method

Heat the olive oil in a frying pan or griddle pan, add the asparagus and cook for around 4 minutes, turning occasionally. Sprinkle the parmesan cheese on top of the asparagus and cook for another couple of minutes or until the cheese has softened. Serve and season with black pepper. Eat straight away, either on its own or with a leafy green salad.

Basil & Lemon Hummus With Celery

Ingredients

200g (7oz) chickpeas (garbanzo beans), drained

8 stalks of celery

2 cloves of garlic

1 handful fresh basil leaves, roughly chopped

Juice of 1 lemon

1 tablespoon olive oil

1 teaspoon sea salt

SERVES 4

94 calories per serving

Method

Place all of the ingredients, except the celery, into a food processor and process until smooth. Serve as a dip for the celery stalks.

Oven Roasted Tomatoes & Feta Cheese

Ingredients

900g (2lb) small tomatoes, halved

75g (3oz) feta cheese, chopped

3 cloves of garlic, finely chopped

1/4 teaspoon chilli flakes

Small handful of fresh thyme leaves, chopped

50mls (2fl oz) olive oil

Sea Salt

Freshly ground black pepper

SERVES 6

812 calories per serving

Method

Place the olive oil, garlic, chilli, salt and pepper into a bowl and mix well. Add in the tomatoes and coat them completely in the oil mixture.

Scatter the tomatoes on a baking sheet, in one single layer with the cut side facing upwards. Place them in the oven and cook at 230C/ 450F for around 30 minutes. Serve with a sprinkle of feta cheese on top. This can be enjoyed hot or cold.

Basil & Tomato Olives

Ingredients

50g (2oz) pitted green olives

1 tablespoon fresh basil, chopped

1 tomato, chopped

1 clove of garlic chopped

Black pepper

SERVES 1

84 calories per serving

Method

Place all of the ingredients into a bowl and mix well. Chill before serving.

Carrot & Basil Soup

Ingredients

450g (1lb) carrots, chopped

3 tablespoons fresh basil, plus extra for garnish

2 onions, chopped

1 courgette, (zucchini)

1 tablespoon olive oil

1200mls (2 pints) hot water

SERVES 4

94 calories per serving

Method

Heat the oil in a saucepan, add the onions and cook for 5 minutes. Add in the carrots and courgette (zucchini) and cook for 5 minutes. Stir in the orange zest and hot water. Reduce the heat and simmer for 10 minutes. Stir in the parsley and orange juice. Using a hand blender or food processor blend the soup until smooth. Re-heat if necessary before serving. Serve with a sprinkling of basil.

Quick Chicken & Red Pepper Soup

Ingredients

100g (3½ oz) cooked chicken, chopped

½ red pepper (bell pepper), sliced

250mls (9 fl oz) chicken stock (broth)

1 teaspoon fresh basil, chopped

1 teaspoon olive oil

SERVES 1

224 calories per serving

Method

Heat the olive oil in a frying pan, add the red pepper (bell pepper) and cook for 3 minutes. Pour in the stock (broth) and add the chicken. Cook for 10-15 minutes. Sprinkle in the basil and serve.

Tomato & Pesto Soup

Ingredients

3 tomatoes

1 stalk of celery, chopped

1 teaspoon pesto sauce

2 teaspoons crème fraîche

360mls (12fl oz) hot stock (broth)

Freshly ground black pepper

SERVES 1

81 calories per serving

Method

Place the tomatoes, celery and pesto into a saucepan and add the water and stock (broth). Cook for 8-10 minutes. Using a hand blender or food processor blitz the soup until it's smooth. Add the crème fraîche and stir well. Season with salt and pepper then serve.

Quick Chicken & Asparagus Soup

Ingredients

2 asparagus stalks, finely chopped

1 small chicken breast, finely chopped

1 small carrot, finely diced

1/2 small courgette (zucchini), finely chopped

250mls (8fl oz) chicken stock (broth)

1/2 teaspoon lemon juice

1 teaspoon olive oil

Freshly ground black pepper

**SERVES
1**

235
calories
per serving

Method

Heat the olive oil in a saucepan, add the chicken and cook it for 5 minutes, stirring occasionally. Pour in the stock (broth) and add the courgette (zucchini), lemon juice, carrot and asparagus. Bring it to the boil, reduce the heat and simmer for 15 minutes. Season and serve.

Fennel & Broccoli Soup

Ingredients

450g (1lb) broccoli, chopped

1 fennel bulb, chopped

1 courgette (zucchini), chopped

1 handful parsley, chopped

1 handful chives, chopped

Sea salt

Freshly ground black pepper

SERVES 4

170 calories per serving

Method

Place the broccoli, leek, courgette (zucchini) and fennel in enough water to cover them and bring to the boil. Simmer for 10-15 minutes or until the vegetables are tender. Stir in the herbs. Using a hand blender or food processor blend until the soup becomes smooth. Add more water if required to adjust the consistency. Season and serve.

Quick Bean
& Parmesan Soup

Ingredients

100g (3½ oz) cannellini beans, drained

3 spring onions (scallions), chopped

1 tomato, de-seeded and chopped

1 small carrot, finely diced

1 clove of garlic, crushed

½ small courgette (zucchini) finely diced

½ teaspoon dried mixed herbs

1 tablespoon Parmesan cheese, grated (shredded)

1 tablespoon tomato purée (paste)

250mls (8fl oz) vegetable stock (broth)

1 teaspoon olive oil

**SERVES
1**

225
calories
per serving

Method

Heat the olive oil in a saucepan, add the carrots, spring onions (scallions), courgette (zucchini) and garlic. Cook for 4 minutes or until the vegetables have softened. Pour in the stock (broth), mixed herbs and the tomato purée (paste). Bring to the boil, reduce the heat and simmer for 10 minutes. Add the beans and tomatoes and warm them completely. Serve the soup with the Parmesan cheese sprinkled on top. Eat straight away.

Beef & Mushroom Soup

Ingredients

50g (2oz) cooked sliced beef, chopped

2 large mushrooms, finely sliced

3 spring onions (scallions) finely chopped

1 stick of celery, finely chopped

1 teaspoon olive oil

250mls (8fl oz) beef stock (broth)

Sea salt

Freshly ground black pepper

SERVES 1

133 calories per serving

Method

Heat the oil in a saucepan, add the mushrooms, spring onions (scallions) and celery and cook for 3-4 minutes. Pour in the stock (broth) and chopped beef. Bring it to the boil, reduce the heat and cook for 10 minutes. Season with salt and pepper. Serve and enjoy.

Creamy Red Pepper Soup

Ingredients

1 red pepper (bell pepper), de-seeded and finely chopped

2 teaspoons crème fraîche

250mls (8fl oz) hot stock (broth)

Sea salt

Freshly ground black pepper

SERVES 1

54 calories per serving

Method

Place the red pepper (bell pepper) into a saucepan and pour in the hot stock (broth). Bring the ingredients to the boil, reduce the heat and simmer for a few minutes until the pepper has softened. Using a hand blender or food processor whizz the soup until smooth. Stir in the crème fraîche and season with salt and pepper. Serve and enjoy.

Vegetable & Chorizo Soup

Ingredients

400g (14oz) tin cannellini beans, drained and rinsed

200g (7oz) chorizo sausage, sliced

3 large carrots, peeled and diced

1 onion, peeled and finely chopped

1 red pepper (bell pepper), chopped

1 green pepper (bell pepper), chopped

1 garlic clove, crushed

1 teaspoon chilli powder

600mls (1 pint) warm vegetable stock (broth)

1 tablespoon olive oil

Salt and freshly ground black pepper

SERVES 4

355 calories per serving

Method

Heat the oil in a large saucepan, add the chorizo and cook for 3 minutes. Remove it and set aside. Add in the onion, garlic and carrots. Cover and cook gently for about 5 minutes, stirring occasionally. Add in the chilli powder and vegetable stock (broth) and bring to the boil. Return the chorizo to the soup and add in the peppers (bell peppers) and cannellini beans and cook for 5 minutes. Season with salt and pepper. Serve into bowls.

Asparagus Soup

Ingredients

375g (12oz) asparagus spears, tough end removed

2 cloves of garlic, chopped

1 handful of spinach leaves

1 tablespoon butter

750mls (1½ pints) vegetable stock (broth)

SERVES 4

64 calories per serving

Method

Heat the butter in a saucepan, add the asparagus and garlic and cook for 4 minutes. Add in the spinach and vegetable stock (broth) and cook for 5 minutes. Using a hand blender or food processor blend the soup until smooth. Serve into bowls.

Broccoli & Cheese Soup

Ingredients

175g (6oz) cheese, grated (shredded)

1 head of broccoli, chopped

1 leek, chopped

1 courgette (zucchini), chopped

1 litre (1½ pints) chicken stock (broth)

150mls (5fl oz) single cream

Sea salt

Freshly ground black pepper

SERVES 4

309 calories per serving

Method

Place the broccoli, leek and courgette (zucchini) in a saucepan and pour in the stock (broth). Bring them to the boil, reduce the heat and simmer for 15 minutes or until the vegetables are tender. Stir in the cream then using a hand blender or food processor blend until the soup becomes smooth. Add a little hot water or stock (broth) if you want to adjust the consistency. Season with salt and pepper and sprinkle with cheese.

MAIN MEALS

Salmon & Pomegranate Salsa

Ingredients

4 salmon fillets

2 medium carrots, finely chopped

1/2 teaspoon sea salt

1/4 teaspoon black pepper

1/8 teaspoon cayenne pepper

1 medium shallot, peeled and thinly sliced

2 medium oranges, peeled and sectioned

1 tablespoon olive oil

Seeds of 2 pomegranates

SERVES 4

427 calories per serving

Method

In a small bowl, mix together the black pepper, sea salt, cayenne pepper and olive oil. Coat the salmon with the mixture. In a separate bowl, combine the carrots, shallot, pomegranate, chives and orange segments. Place the salmon under a hot grill (broiler) and cook for around 5 minutes on each side, until completely cooked and the fish flakes apart. Serve the salmon and spoon some salsa on top. Enjoy straight away.

Tomato & Herb Stuffed Chicken

Ingredients

450g (1lb) chicken breasts

75g (3oz) black olives, finely chopped

50g (2oz) butter, softened

6 sundried tomatoes, finely chopped

3 cloves of garlic, crushed

1 tablespoon capers

1 teaspoon dried oregano

1 teaspoon dried basil

Sea salt

Freshly ground black pepper

SERVES 4

333 calories per serving

Method

Place the olives, tomatoes, garlic, dried herbs and capers into a bowl and stir. Add in the softened butter and capers and mix well. Make an incision in each chicken breast to make a pocket for the butter mixture. Spoon the mixture inside each of the chicken breasts. Season with salt and pepper and wrap each one in tin foil. Transfer them to the oven and cook at 190C/375F for 25 minutes or until cooked.

Spicy Meatballs & Yogurt Dip

Ingredients

450g (1lb) minced turkey (or beef)
50g (2oz) ground almonds
3 tablespoons harissa paste
1 tablespoon tomato purée (paste)
1 garlic clove, crushed
Juice of 1 lemon
1 egg
2 tablespoons extra virgin olive oil

FOR THE DIP:
200g (7oz) plain yogurt (unflavoured)
12 mint leaves, finely chopped

SERVES 4

344 calories per serving

Method

In a bowl, combine the turkey with 2 tablespoons of harissa paste, the almonds, garlic, lemon juice and egg and mix really well. Scoop portions of the mixture out with a spoon and shape into balls. Cover and refrigerate for 40 minutes. Heat the oil in a frying pan, add a tablespoon of harissa paste and tomato purée (paste) and stir. Add the meatballs and cook for 7-8 minutes, turning occasionally until thoroughly cooked. In the meantime, combine the yogurt and mint and mix well. Skewer each meatball with a cocktail stick and serve ready to be dipped in the yogurt. Enjoy.

Mustard Turkey & Mashed Butter Beans

Ingredients

400g (14oz) tin of butter beans, drained and rinsed

50g (2oz) fresh spinach leaves

2 turkey fillets

2 tablespoons crème fraîche

1 garlic clove, crushed

1 teaspoon wholegrain mustard

Juice of ½ lime

Sea salt

Freshly ground black pepper

SERVES 2

411 calories per serving

Method

Place the lime juice and mustard in a bowl and mix together. Add the turkey steaks and coat them well. Place the turkey steaks under a hot grill (broiler) and cook for 5-6 minutes on each side until thoroughly cooked. In the meantime, place the butter beans in a saucepan and add in the garlic and crème fraîche. Season with salt and pepper. Warm the beans thoroughly. Remove the beans from the heat and mash them. Scatter the spinach leaves onto a plate. Spoon the mash on top and add the turkey steak.

Slow Cooked Chicken Cacciatore

Ingredients

250g (9 oz) mushrooms, sliced

4 chicken breasts

2 x 400g (14oz) tins of chopped tomatoes

2 green peppers (bell peppers) chopped

2 cloves garlic, chopped

1 onion, finely chopped

1 tablespoon tomato paste (purée)

1 teaspoon dried basil

SERVES 4

225 calories per serving

Method

Place all ingredients in the slow cooker and stir them well. Place the lid on the slow cooker and cook for 6-7 hours. Serve with mashed cauliflower, salad or roast vegetables.

Roast Lemon & Herb Chicken

Ingredients

6 sprigs of oregano, stalk removed

3 large handfuls rocket (arugula)

1 large whole chicken

2 tablespoons olive oil

Juice of 2 lemons

Sea salt

Freshly ground black pepper

1 sliced lemon

SERVES 4

244 calories per serving

Method

Place the oregano, lemon juice, olive oil, salt and pepper into a large bowl and mix well. Place the chicken into the marinade. Cover and chill in the fridge for at least 1 hour or overnight if you can. Place the chicken and marinade juices into a roasting tin and cook at 180C/360 for 1 ½ hours or until the juices of the chicken run clear when tested with a skewer. Carve the chicken and serve with slices of lemon and fresh rocket leaves. Alternatively you can serve the chicken with fresh steamed vegetables or roasted cauliflower.

Tomato & Courgette (Zucchini) Bake

Ingredients

75g (3oz) ground almonds (almond meal/almond flour)

50g (2oz) Parmesan cheese, grated (shredded)

4 tomatoes, sliced

4 courgettes (zucchinis), sliced

1 teaspoon olive oil

Sea salt

Freshly ground black pepper

SERVES 4

218 calories per serving

Method

Grease an ovenproof dish with the olive oil. Place a layer of tomatoes on the bottom of the dish. Now add a layer of courgette (zucchini). Season with salt and pepper. Sprinkle the ground almonds (almond meal/almond flour) over the top. Add a sprinkling of Parmesan cheese. Transfer it to the oven and bake at 180C/360F for 15-20 minutes until the top is golden.

Lemon & Almond Crumbed Prawns

Ingredients

400g (14oz) cooked frozen prawns (shrimps), shelled and defrosted

75g (3oz) ground almonds (almond meal/almond flour)

Zest of a lemon, grated (shredded)

1 tablespoon olive oil

Sea salt

White pepper

SERVES 4

215 calories per serving

Method

Place the ground almonds (almond meal/almond flour) into a bowl. Add in the lemon zest and season with salt and pepper. Add the prawns to the bowl and coat them in the almond mixture. Heat the olive oil in a frying pan. Add the prawns and cook them for around 2 minutes on each side. Serve with a slice of lemon or you can add a dollop of guacamole or mayonnaise. Enjoy.

Paprika Pork Skewers

Ingredients

400g (14oz) pork steaks, cut into bite-sized chunks

1 tablespoon tomato purée (paste)

1 garlic clove, crushed

1 red pepper (bell pepper), cut into chunks

1 onion, cut into chunks

1 teaspoon smoked paprika

1 tablespoon lemon juice

1 tablespoon olive oil

SERVES 4

227 calories per serving

Method

Place the paprika, tomato purée (paste), lemon juice, garlic and olive oil into a bowl and mix well. Add the pork pieces to the mixture and coat them thoroughly. Allow them to marinate for at least 1 hour. Thread the marinated pork, red pepper (bell pepper) and onion on skewers, alternating the ingredients. Place the skewers under a pre-heated grill (broiler) and cook for 9-10 minutes, turning during cooking until they are cooked through.

Turkey & Chickpea Balls

Ingredients

400g (14oz) tinned chick-peas (garbanzo beans), drained

250g (9oz) turkey mince (ground turkey)

50g (2oz) chickpea flour (garbanzo bean flour/gram flour)

2 garlic cloves, finely chopped

2 tablespoons olive oil

1 teaspoon cumin

1/2 onion, chopped

1/2 teaspoon baking powder

Sea salt

Freshly ground black pepper

SERVES 4

322
calories
per serving

Method

Place all of the ingredients, except the oil, into a food processor and mix until everything is well combined. Transfer the mixture to a bowl, cover it and chill in the fridge for around 30 minutes. When the mixture has firmed up slightly, take a spoonful of the mixture and using wet hands, shape it into balls. Repeat for the remaining mixture. Heat the olive oil in a frying pan, add the balls and cook them for 12-15 minutes, turning frequently until cooked through. Serve with guacamole or mayonnaise and salad.

Chorizo Stir-Fry

Ingredients

200g (7oz) chorizo sausage, chopped

6 large kale leaves

1 onion, chopped

1 red pepper (bell pepper), chopped

Sea salt

Freshly ground black pepper

SERVES 2

451 calories per serving

Method

Heat a frying pan, add the sausage and cook for 5 minutes or until completely brown. Add in the onion and cook for 4 minutes. Next, add in the kale and red pepper (bell pepper) and cook until the vegetables have softened. Season with salt and pepper. Serve and eat immediately.

Slow-Cooked Ratatouille

Ingredients

225g (8oz) cherry tomatoes
3 medium sized courgettes (zucchinis)
3 cloves of garlic, chopped
1 onion, peeled and chopped
1 aubergine (eggplant) chopped
2 red peppers (bell peppers), de-seeded and chopped
1 teaspoon dried Herbs de Provence
175mls (6fl oz) vegetable stock (broth)
A handful of fresh basil, chopped
1-2 teaspoons cornflour
2 teaspoons olive oil

SERVES 4

111 calories per serving

Method

Heat the olive oil in a frying pan, add the chopped onion and cook for 5 minutes. Transfer the onions to a slow cooker. Add all the remaining ingredients to the slow cooker, apart from the cornflour and the basil. Cook on high for 3 hours. Mix the cornflour with a tablespoon of cold water and stir it into the ratatouille. Cook for another 30 minutes. Stir in the fresh basil before serving.

Spiced Citrus & Olive Pork

Ingredients

150g (5oz) pitted green olives
450g (1lb) pork steaks, cut into chunks
2 cloves of garlic, crushed
2 lemons, sliced and seeds removed
1 onion, finely chopped
1 teaspoon ground ginger
1 teaspoon ground coriander (cilantro)
2 teaspoons turmeric
1 tablespoon olive oil
450mls (15fl oz) chicken stock (broth)
Handful of fresh parsley, chopped
Sea salt
Freshly ground black pepper

SERVES 4

304 calories per serving

Method

Heat the oil in a large saucepan. Add the onion and cook for 5 minutes until it softens. Add the garlic, ginger, coriander (cilantro) and turmeric and cook for 1 minute. Add the pork pieces and cook for 5 minutes, stirring occasionally. Add the sliced lemons and the stock (broth). Season with salt and pepper. Bring it to the boil, reduce the heat and simmer gently for 30 minutes. Add the olives and cook for a further 3 minutes. Stir in the parsley. This dish can be served with salad, cauliflower rice or courgette spaghetti.

Smoked Salmon & Pesto 'Spaghetti'

Ingredients

75g (3oz) smoked salmon, sliced

4 medium courgettes (zucchinis)

1 tablespoon pesto sauce

2 lemon wedges

SERVES 2

307 calories per serving

Method

Prepare the courgette (zucchini) by using a spiraliser to create strips of courgette (zucchini) If you don't have a spiraliser, use a vegetable peeler and cut the strips into thin spaghetti-like lengths. Place the courgette strips into a steamer and cook for 3-4 minutes until they have softened. Once it has cooked, stir the pesto into the courgette (zucchini). Serve it into bowls and top if off with the smoked salmon. Squeeze a piece of lemon over the top and enjoy.

Tuna Casserole

Ingredients

4 tuna steaks

2 red onions, chopped

2 stalks of celery

2 x 400g (2 x 14oz) tins of chopped tomatoes

2 cloves of garlic

1 tablespoon olive oil

1 lemon, thinly sliced

1 tablespoon tomato purée (paste)

2 tablespoons fresh oregano, chopped

Sea salt

Freshly ground black pepper

SERVES 4

229 calories per serving

Method

Heat the oil in a saucepan and add the celery, garlic and onions and fry for 5 minutes until the vegetables have softened. Add in the tinned tomatoes, oregano, tomato purée (paste) and lemon slices. Bring to the boil and simmer, stirring, for 5 minutes. Season with salt and pepper. Place the fish in the tomato mixture. Simmer gently for 12-14 minutes until the fish is cooked. Serve the fish onto plates and pour the sauce on top. Garnish with a little oregano.

Halloumi Skewers

Ingredients

200g (7oz) halloumi cheese, cut into 2cm (1 inch) chunks

8 button mushrooms

1 red pepper (bell pepper), cut into chunks

1 red onion, cut into chunks

1 clove of garlic, crushed

1 tablespoon olive oil

Juice of 1 lime

Freshly ground black pepper

A small handful of fresh chopped coriander (cilantro)

SERVES 2

424 calories per serving

Method

Place the olive oil, coriander (cilantro), garlic and lime into a bowl and mix well. Season with black pepper. Add the halloumi, mushrooms, onion and red pepper (bell pepper) and allow it to marinate for around 1 hour. Thread the ingredients onto skewers alternating them until everything has been used up. Place the kebabs under a preheated grill (broiler) for 10-12 minutes, turning once halfway through. Serve with a green leafy salad.

Fried Avocados

Ingredients

25g (1oz) ground almonds (almond meal/almond flour)

1 ripe avocado

1 egg

1/2 teaspoon onion powder

1/4 teaspoon chilli powder

1/4 teaspoon sea salt

1 teaspoon olive oil

SERVES 1

538 calories per serving

Method

Halve the avocado and remove the stone and the skin. Cut it into slices of around 1-2cms thick. Whisk the egg in a bowl and set aside. Place the ground almonds (almond meal/almond flour) into a bowl and add the onion powder, chilli and salt. Dip the avocado slices in the beaten egg and then dip it in the almond mixture, coating them well. Coat a baking sheet with olive oil and lay the avocado slices on it. Transfer it to the oven and cook for 15-20 minutes at 180C/360F, turning the slices half way through and cooking until slightly golden. Serve and eat straight away.

Slow Cooked Beans & Pancetta

Ingredients

2 x 400g (2 x 14oz) tins of cannellini beans, drained

2 x 400g (2 x 14oz) tins of chopped tomatoes

25g (1oz) butter

4 strips of pancetta, finely chopped

1 large onion, finely chopped

250mls (8fl oz) vegetable stock (broth)

SERVES 4

306 calories per serving

Method

Heat the butter in a frying pan, add the onion and pancetta and cook for a few minutes until the onion has softened. Transfer them to a slow cooker. Add the tomatoes, beans and vegetable stock (broth). Cook on low for 7 hours. Serve on their own or as a side dish. Makes a great sugar-free alternative to tinned baked beans.

Chicken, Chorizo & Vegetable Casserole

Ingredients

450g (1lb) skinless chicken thighs

400g (14oz) tinned chopped tomatoes

225g (8oz) chickpeas (garbanzo beans), drained

100g (3½ oz) chorizo sausage, cut into bite-sized chunks

3 cloves garlic, chopped

2 red peppers (bell peppers), chopped

2 teaspoons ground coriander (cilantro)

½ teaspoon smoked paprika

1 onion, peeled and chopped

200mls (7fl oz) chicken stock (broth)

1 tablespoon olive oil

Sea salt

Freshly ground black pepper

SERVES 4

428 calories per serving

Method

Heat the oil in a frying pan, add the chicken thighs and cook until golden. Remove them from the pan and set aside. Add the chorizo to the oil and cook for 2 minutes. Add in the onions, garlic, red peppers (bell peppers) and coriander (cilantro) and cook for 3 minutes. Pour in the chopped tomatoes, smoked paprika, chickpeas (garbanzo beans) and the stock (broth) and add the chicken thighs. Bring it to the boil and simmer for 25 minutes. Season with salt and pepper. Serve with roast vegetables.

Roasted Sardines With Herb Crust

Ingredients

450g (1lb) fresh sardines, rinsed and patted dry

2 cloves of garlic, finely chopped

2 teaspoons mustard

1 tablespoon dried oregano

1/2 teaspoon paprika

1/2 teaspoon sea salt

3 tablespoons olive oil

Juice of 1/2 lemon

A small handful of parsley, chopped

SERVES 4

296 calories per serving

Method

Place all of the ingredients, except the sardines and parsley, into a large bowl and mix well. Add in the sardines and coat them well in the mixture. Place the sardines in a casserole dish in a single layer. Roast them in the oven at 220C/440F. Sprinkle them with parsley. Serve on their own or with a heap of green salad or roast vegetables.

Pulled Chicken Wraps

Ingredients

4 skinless chicken breasts

4 large tomatoes, roughly chopped

4 medium sized onions, peeled and chopped

4 cloves of garlic, chopped

2 teaspoon ground ginger

1/2 teaspoon ground cinnamon

2 teaspoons fresh basil, chopped

1 teaspoon chilli powder

1 teaspoon cloves

1 iceberg or romaine lettuce, leaves separated

100mls (3 1/2 fl oz) hot water

SERVES 4

244
calories
per serving

Method

Place all of the ingredients, except the lettuce, into a slow cooker and stir well. Cook on low for around 6 hours. Use a fork to pull the chicken into shreds and mix it thoroughly with the other ingredients. To serve, spoon the pulled chicken mixture into lettuce leaves and fold them over. Alternatively, transfer it to a serving dish for everyone to help themselves.

Sundried Tomato Stuffed Chicken

Ingredients

450g (1lb) chicken breasts

75g (3oz) black olives, finely chopped

50g (2oz) butter, softened

6 sundried tomatoes, finely chopped

3 cloves of garlic, crushed

1 tablespoon capers

1 teaspoon dried oregano

1 teaspoon dried basil

Sea salt

Freshly ground black pepper

SERVES 4

333 calories per serving

Method

Place the olives, tomatoes, garlic, dried herbs and capers into a bowl and stir. Add in the softened butter and capers and mix well. Make an incision in each chicken breast to make a pocket for the butter mixture. Spoon the mixture inside each of the chicken breasts. Season with salt and pepper and wrap each one in tin foil. Transfer them to the oven and cook at 190C/375F for 25 minutes or until cooked.

Balsamic Roast Vegetables

Ingredients

100g (3oz) red chicory (or if unavailable use yellow)

5 stalks of celery, chopped

4 tomatoes, chopped

2 red onions, chopped

3 sweet potatoes, peeled and chopped

1 bird's-eye chilli, de-seeded and chopped

100g (3½ oz) kale, chopped

2 tablespoons fresh coriander (cilantro) chopped

2 tablespoons fresh parsley, chopped

3 tablespoons olive oil

2 tablespoons balsamic vinegar

1 teaspoon mustard

SERVES 4

244 calories per serving

Method

Place the olive oil, balsamic, mustard, parsley and coriander into a bowl and mix well. Toss the remaining ingredients into the dressing and season with salt and pepper. Transfer the vegetables to an ovenproof dish and cook in the oven at 200C/400F for 45 minutes.

Cod With Tomato & Olives

Ingredients

400g (14oz) tin of chopped tomatoes

75g (3oz) pitted black olives, sliced

4 cod fillets

1 onion, chopped

2 cloves of garlic, crushed

2 tablespoons olive oil

100mls (3½ fl oz) vegetable or chicken stock (broth)

Handful of fresh parsley

SERVES 4

223 calories per serving

Method

Heat the oil in a frying pan, add the onions and garlic and cook for 5 minutes. Add in chopped tomatoes, parsley, olives and stock. Bring it to the boil and simmer for 5 minutes. Add the cod fillets in the sauce and simmer gently for 5-6 minutes or until the fish is white and thoroughly cooked.

Rosemary Chicken & Roast Vegetables

Ingredients

250g (9oz) cherry tomatoes, halved

4 chicken breasts

1 aubergine (eggplant, roughly chopped

2 courgettes (zucchinis), roughly chopped

2 red peppers (bell peppers), sliced

1 green pepper (bell pepper), sliced

4 sprigs of fresh rosemary

2 cloves of garlic, chopped

2 tablespoons olive oil

SERVES 4

318 calories per serving

Method

In a large ovenproof dish, spread the aubergine (eggplant), tomatoes, courgettes, (zucchinis) and peppers (bell peppers) with 2 sprigs of rosemary, 1 clove of garlic and a tablespoon of olive oil. Transfer it to the oven and cook at 200C/400F for 5 minutes. In the meantime, mix the remaining garlic, rosemary and olive oil in a bowl. Make an incision in the chicken breasts and spread some of the mixture into each one. Once the vegetables have been in for 5 minutes, add the chicken breasts to the dish. Return it to the oven and cook for another 20 minutes or until the chicken is thoroughly cooked.

Tomato & Pesto Chicken

Ingredients

200g (7oz) tinned chopped tomatoes

25g (1oz) sundried tomatoes, chopped

2 teaspoons pesto

1 teaspoon pine nuts

1 chicken breast

1 small handful of fresh basil, chopped

1 large handful of fresh mixed lettuce leaves

SERVES 1

363 calories per serving

Method

Place the tinned tomatoes in an ovenproof dish and add in the sundried tomatoes and basil and stir well. Coat both sides of the chicken breast with the pesto then lay it on top of the tomatoes. Cook in the oven at 200C/400F for around 30 minutes or until the chicken is completely cooked. Scatter the salad leaves onto a plate. Serve the chicken on top with a scattering of pine nuts.

Spiced Quinoa & Chickpea Falafels

Ingredients

400g (14oz) tin of chickpeas
200g (7oz) quinoa, cooked
3 spring onions (scallions), finely chopped
2 teaspoons ground coriander (cilantro)
1 teaspoon ground turmeric
1 teaspoon ground cumin
1/2 red pepper, finely diced
2 tablespoons water
2 tablespoons olive oil
Juice of 1/2 lemon

MAKES 4

34 calories each

Method

Place the chickpeas into a blender and process until smooth then transfer it to a large bowl. Heat the olive oil in a frying pan, add the spring onions (scallions) red pepper and celery and cook it for 5 minutes until they have softened. Add them to the bowl with the chickpeas. Add in the quinoa and mix until all of the ingredients are thoroughly combined. Shape the mixture into bite-size balls. You can wet your hands slightly and/or or add a tablespoon or two of water to the mixture to help shape it. Lay them out on a greased baking tray. Transfer them to the oven and bake at 180C/360F for 20 minutes or until golden.

Broccoli
& Bean Bites

Ingredients

250g (9oz) cannellini beans, drained

150g (5oz) broccoli, cut into florets

2 tablespoons ground almonds

1 tablespoon tahini paste

1 tablespoon lemon juice

1 egg

1 teaspoon fresh parsley

**SERVES
4**

156
calories
per serving

Method

Steam the broccoli for 5 minutes. Place all of the ingredients into a blender and process until the mixture is smooth. Shape the mixture into ball shapes and place them on a lined baking tray. Cook them in the oven at 180C/360F for 25 minutes.

Sirloin Steak & Garlic Prawns

Ingredients

225g (7oz) peeled raw prawns (shrimps)

4 tablespoons crème fraîche

2 sirloin steaks (approx. 100g each)

2 tablespoons butter

1 tablespoon olive oil

3 cloves of garlic, chopped

Sea salt

Freshly ground black pepper

SERVES 2

400 calories per serving

Method

Sprinkle salt on each side of the steaks. Heat the oil in a frying pan, add the steaks and cook for 3-4 minutes, (or longer if you like them well done) turning once. Remove them from the pan and set them aside and keep them warm. Heat the butter to the pan, add the prawns (shrimps) garlic and crème fraîche and cook for until the prawns are completely pink. Season with salt and pepper. Serve the steaks onto plates and spoon the prawns and sauce over the top. Eat straight away.

Halloumi, Pine Nut & Vegetable Bake

Ingredients

350g (1lb) halloumi cheese, thickly sliced

25g (1oz) pine nuts

8 cherry tomatoes, halved

3 cloves of garlic, chopped

2 onions, peeled and chopped

1 yellow pepper (bell pepper), deseeded and chopped

1 red pepper (bell pepper), deseeded and chopped

1 handful of fresh basil, chopped

1 handful of fresh parsley, chopped

1 tablespoon olive oil

2 teaspoons paprika

SERVES 4

378 calories per serving

Method

Preheat the oven to 200C/400F. Scatter the tomatoes, onions, peppers and garlic into a roasting tin. Coat them in paprika and olive oil. Toss them well in the mixture. Lay the halloumi on top of the vegetables. Transfer it to the oven and cook for 25 minutes or until the halloumi is golden. Add in the parsley, basil and pine nuts and serve.

Lemon Salmon & Spinach

Ingredients

50g (2oz) spinach leaves

2 salmon fillets

2 tablespoons fresh parsley, chopped

2 tablespoons olive oil

1 clove of garlic

Juice of 1 lemon

Freshly ground black pepper

SERVES 2

402 calories per serving

Method

Mix together the lemon juice, 2 tablespoons olive oil, garlic and parsley and season with pepper. Place the fish on a plate and lightly coat it with a tablespoon of the lemon & parsley mixture. Heat a frying pan and add the salmon. Cook for 3-4 minutes on each side and check that it's completely cooked. Scatter the spinach leaves onto plates. Serve the fish on top and spoon over the remaining lemon and parsley dressing. Enjoy.

Mushroom Stuffed Peppers

Ingredients

400g (14oz) tin of cannellini beans, drained
4 large mushrooms, chopped
3 cloves of garlic, chopped
2 red peppers (bell peppers), top removed and deseeded
2 yellow peppers (bell peppers), top removed and deseeded
1 onion, peeled and finely chopped
2 eggs
1 teaspoon paprika
A handful of fresh basil
Sea salt
Freshly ground black pepper

SERVES 4

183 calories per serving

Method

Place the beans, mushrooms, eggs, garlic, onion, basil and paprika into a bowl and mix well. Season with salt and pepper. Scoop some of the mixture into each of the peppers and place the lid back onto the peppers. Place the peppers onto a baking tray. Transfer them to the oven at 180C/ 360F for 20-25 minutes. Serve and eat straight away.

Mozzarella & Aubergine Bake

Ingredients

50g (2oz) mozzarella cheese, grated (shredded)

4 large ripe tomatoes

2 ripe aubergines (eggplants)

1 tablespoons olive oil

A small handful of fresh basil, chopped

SERVES 4

99 calories per serving

Method

Cut the tomatoes into slices and set aside. Thinly slice the aubergines (eggplants) and place them under a hot grill (broiler). Brush with olive oil and cook for 15 minutes, turning once. Place the tomato slices and aubergine slices in an oven-proof dish, alternating between slices of each. Cover with the grated mozzarella. Transfer to the oven and bake at 200C/400F for 15 minutes, or until the cheese is golden. Sprinkle with fresh basil and enjoy straight away.

SWEET TREATS

Macadamia & Chocolate Yogurt

Ingredients

100g (3½ oz) plain Greek yogurt

1 teaspoon 100% cocoa powder

6 macadamia nuts, chopped

SERVES 1

227 calories per serving

Method

Place the yogurt and cocoa powder into a bowl and stir until completely combined. Sprinkle the chopped nuts over the top. Serve and enjoy!

Chocolate Cashew Truffles

Ingredients

14 pitted dates, finely chopped

2 tablespoons 100% cocoa powder

125g (4oz) unsalted cashew nuts, finely chopped

1 tablespoon coconut oil

50g (2oz) ground almonds

MAKES 12

122
calories
per serving

Method

Place the dry ingredients into a bowl and mix them well. Add in the coconut oil and combine it thoroughly. Shape the mixture into balls and store them in an airtight container. Keep refrigerated.

Vanilla Mug Cake

Ingredients

2 teaspoons ground flaxseeds (linseeds)

2 tablespoons ground almonds (almond meal/almond flour)

1 egg

1/2 teaspoon vanilla extract

1/2 teaspoon baking powder

1/2 teaspoon stevia (or to taste)

1 teaspoon coconut oil

Pinch of salt

SERVES 1

343 calories per serving

Method

Place all the ingredients into a large mug or a microwaveable bowl and mix well. Cook in the microwave for 30 seconds. Remove it and stir. Return it to the microwave and cook for another 30 seconds, remove and return it to the microwave and cook for another 30 seconds. Chill in the fridge before serving.

Banana Frappuccino

Ingredients

1 frozen banana

175mls (6fl oz) almond milk

1 teaspoon instant coffee

1 teaspoon 100% cocoa powder

½-1 teaspoon stevia power (optional)

Method

Toss all of the ingredients into a blender and blitz until smooth. Drink it straight away and enjoy!

Pistachio & Raspberry Fool

Ingredients

100g (3½ oz) plain (unflavoured) Greek yogurt

100g (3½ oz) raspberries

10 pistachio nuts, chopped

Zest and juice of ½ a lime

SERVES 2

200 calories per serving

Method

Place the raspberries into a blender and puree until smooth. Place the yogurt, lime zest and juice into the raspberry purée. Stir but don't mix it completely, aim for a swirled affect. Spoon the yogurt and raspberry mixture into 2 serving glasses or bowls. Top it with the pistachio nuts and serve.

Whipped Yogurt, Apples & Walnuts

Ingredients

50g (2oz) chopped walnuts

2 apples, peeled, cored and cubed

5g (½ oz) butter

½ teaspoon ground cinnamon

350mls (12fl oz) plain Greek yogurt

125mls (4fl oz) whipping cream (heavy cream)

SERVES 4

351 calories per serving

Method

Place the yogurt, honey and cream in a bowl and whisk it until it thickens into soft peaks. Heat the butter in a frying pan and add the apples. Cook them for around 10 minutes or until they have softened. Add in the cinnamon and stir well. Set the mixture aside to cool a little. Spoon the yogurt mixture into serving bowls and spoon the apples on top. Sprinkle with walnuts and enjoy.

You may also be interested in other titles by
Erin Rose Publishing
which are available in both paperback and ebook.

🕐 **Quick Start Guides**

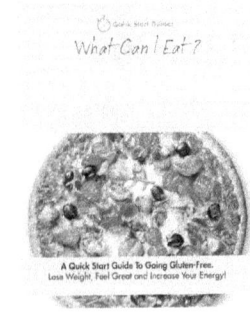

What Can I Eat?
SUGAR FREE DIET
A Quick Start Guide To Quitting Sugar, Lose Weight, Feel Great and Increase Your Energy!

The Essential
SUGAR FREE DIET COOKBOOK
A Quick Start Guide To Sugar Free Cooking Over 100 New and Delicious Sugar-Free Recipes!

The Essential
SUGAR FREE FAMILY COOKBOOK
A Quick Start Guide To Helping Your Family Quit Sugar

The Essential
SUGAR FREE DESSERTS RECIPE BOOK

The Essential
SUGAR FREE SLOW COOKER Recipe Book

The Essential
SUGAR FREE DIET Meals For One

The Essential
BLOOD SUGAR DIET RECIPE BOOK

the New Essential
BLOOD SUGAR DIET COOKBOOK
A Quick Start Guide To Balancing Your Blood Sugar Through Diet, Improve Your Health and Lose Weight

Family Favourites
A Quick Start Guide To Help Your Family Get Healthier

The Essential
BLOOD SUGAR DIET 15 Minute Meals

The Essential
BLOOD SUGAR DIET MEALS FOR ONE
A Quick Start Guide To Cooking On The Blood Sugar Diet Over 80 Easy And Delicious Calorie Counted Recipes For One

BLOOD SUGAR DIET Recipes For Life
A Quick Start Guide To The Blood Sugar Diet

The
LOW CARB HIGH FAT DIET

The Essential
LOW CARB HIGH FAT DIET COOKBOOK
A Quick Start Guide To Low Carb High Fat Cooking

The Essential
LOW CARB DIET MEALS FOR ONE
A Quick Start Guide To Cooking Low Carb Meals For One

What Can I Eat?
A Quick Start Guide To Going Gluten-Free, Lose Weight, Feel Great and Increase Your Energy!

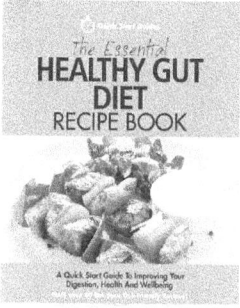

The Essential HEALTHY GUT DIET RECIPE BOOK

A Quick Start Guide To Improving Your Digestion, Health And Wellbeing

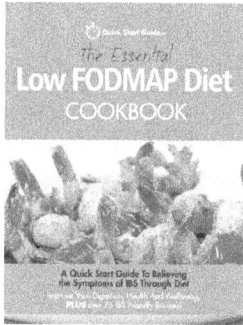

the Essential Low FODMAP Diet COOKBOOK

A Quick Start Guide To Relieving the Symptoms of IBS Through Diet

Improve Your Digestion, Health And Wellbeing
PLUS over 75 IBS Friendly Recipes

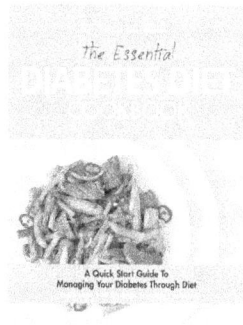

the Essential DIABETES DIET COOKBOOK

A Quick Start Guide To Managing Your Diabetes Through Diet

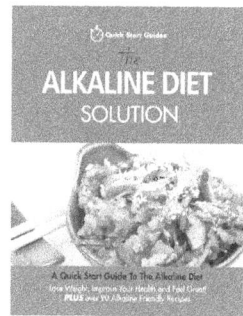

The ALKALINE DIET SOLUTION

A Quick Start Guide To The Alkaline Diet
Lose Weight, Improve Your Health and Feel Great
PLUS over 90 Alkaline Friendly Recipes

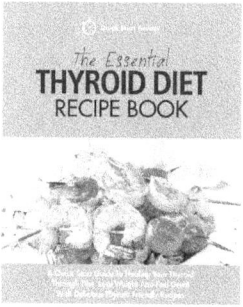

The Essential THYROID DIET RECIPE BOOK

A Quick Start Guide to Healing Your Thyroid
Restore Your Good Health And Feel Great
With Delicious Thyroid Friendly Recipes

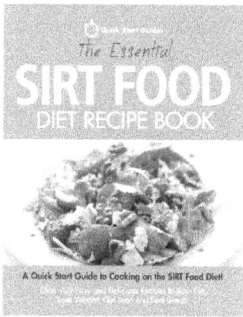

The Essential SIRT FOOD DIET RECIPE BOOK

A Quick Start Guide to Cooking on the SIRT Food Diet

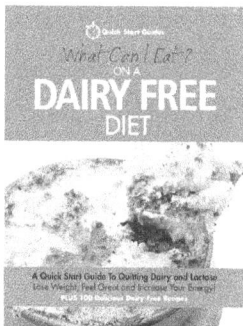

What Can I Eat? ON A DAIRY FREE DIET

A Quick Start Guide To Quitting Dairy and Lactose
Lose Weight, Feel Great and Increase Your Energy!
PLUS 100 Delicious Dairy-Free Recipes

LOWER CHOLESTEROL DIET

A Quick Start Guide To Lower Cholesterol

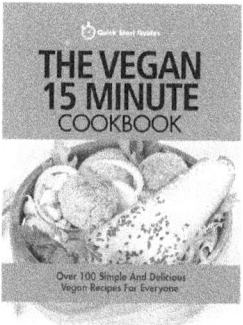

THE VEGAN 15 MINUTE COOKBOOK

Over 100 Simple And Delicious Vegan Recipes For Everyone

The Essential ROASTING TIN COOKBOOK

Over 80 Easy And Delicious One Dish, No-Fuss Oven Recipes

Blood Sugar Diet Diary

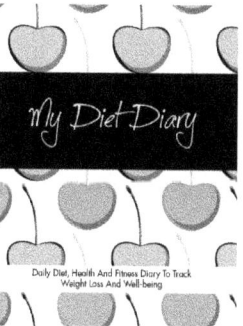

My Diet Diary

Daily Diet, Health And Fitness Diary To Track Weight Loss And Well-being

Low FODMAP Diet Diary

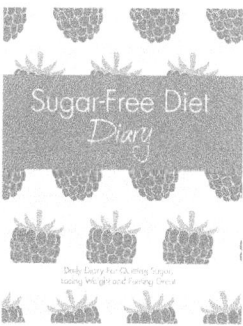

Sugar-Free Diet Diary

Daily Diary For Quitting Sugar, Losing Weight and Feeling Great

FOOD Diary

www.ingramcontent.com/pod-product-compliance
Lightning Source LLC
Chambersburg PA
CBHW081257040426
42452CB00014B/2538